THE MYSTERY
OF THE
ROSARY

Our Lady of the Rosary

The Mystery of the Rosary

By
Rev. Marc Tremeau, O.P.

CATHOLIC BOOK PUBLISHING CORP.
NEW JERSEY

NIHIL OBSTAT: Garrett Fitzgerald, S.J., S.T.L.
Censor Deputatus

IMPRIMATUR: ✠ Joseph T. O'Keefe, D.D.
Vicar General, Archdiocese of New York

Dedicated to ST. JOSEPH
Patron of the Universal Church

This book was especially commissioned by Catholic Book Publishing Corp. Father Marc Tremeau, a world-famous specialist on the Rosary, wrote it in French and it was published by C.L.D. Publications as *Le Mystère du Rosaire*. The readable English translation is the work of Rev. John A. Otto.

(T-105)

CONTENTS

Chapter 1

GENERAL NOTION OF THE ROSARY

THE Rosary, in simplest definition, is a chain of prayer beads. The links connecting the beads, even as the beads themselves, may be made of various material. Most commonly, however, the beads are strung on wire loops.

Prayer beads of one kind or another are used not only by Catholics. We find them, for example, among Brahmins, Buddhists, and Moslems.

The complete Catholic Rosary consists of twenty decades of beads. Ordinarily, when we speak of praying a Rosary, we mean a set of five decades of smaller beads, separated by a larger one. Attached as a sort of introduction to the string of five decades is a chainlet comprising, in order, a cross, a larger bead, three smaller ones, and another larger one.

When we pray the Rosary we begin at the cross, with the Sign of the Cross. Then we say the Apostles' Creed, which is followed by an Our Father at the first larger bead, and three Hail Marys at the three smaller ones, and then a "Glory Be to the Father."

After this introduction we come to the Rosary proper, the five decades. Each decade is prayed as follows: an Our Father at the larger bead that introduces it, a Hail Mary at each of the ten smaller beads, and a "Glory Be to the Father" at the end of the decade. (More

6

simply, the larger beads of the Rosary are for the Our Father, the smaller ones for the Hail Marys.)

At the end of the Rosary the "Hail, Holy Queen" may be said. This is a praiseworthy practice, but it is not essential to the Rosary.

Recitation of Treasured Prayers

The prayers used in the Rosary are among the most treasured of the Catholic world. The Our Father was taught us by Jesus himself. Concise and profound, it has no equal. We shall never finish exploring its lessons. Commentaries produced throughout the centuries are numberless.

The Hail Mary consists of two parts. The first has words of the Archangel Gabriel spoken to Mary at the Annunciation (Lk 1:28), and words by Elizabeth addressed to Mary visiting her (Lk 1:42). The second part, a prayer of petition to Mary, was first introduced by St. Bernardine of Siena, about 1440. The Hail Mary, like the Our Father, overflows with meaning for the Christian life. Said with deep faith and proper understanding, it too is proof against monotony.

The other prayers of the Rosary are similarly sacred. The Apostles' Creed, ancient and enduring, is a profession of the Catholic faith. The Sign of the Cross and the "Glory Be to the Father" honor the deepest mystery of our faith, the Most Blessed Trinity.

Meditation on the Mysteries of Christ

The Rosary, however, is more than saying the prayers. It is also, and most importantly, a means of meditating on the joyful, the luminous, the sorrowful, and the glorious mysteries in the life of Jesus and Mary.

The joyful mysteries revolve around the great wonder of the Incarnation. This is a mystery in the strict sense of the word. Under the joyful mysteries are:

1. The Annunciation of the Archangel Gabriel to Mary.
2. The Visitation of Mary to Elizabeth.
3. The Birth of Jesus at Bethlehem.
4. The Presentation of Jesus in the Temple.
5. The Finding of Jesus in the Temple.

The luminous mysteries added by Pope John Paul II in his Apostolic Letter of October 16, 2002 recall to our mind important events of the public ministry of Christ. This group includes:

1. The Baptism of Jesus.
2. The Wedding at Cana.
3. The Proclamation of the Kingdom.
4. The Transfiguration of Our Lord.
5. The Institution of the Eucharist.

The sorrowful mysteries focus on the Passion of our Lord, i.e., his redemptive suffering and death. Under this group are:

1. The Agony of Jesus in the Garden.
2. The Scourging at the Pillar.
3. The Crowning of Jesus with Thorns.
4. The Carrying of the Cross by Jesus to Calvary.
5. The Crucifixion and Death of Jesus.

The glorious mysteries offer for our meditation the promise of future glory and resurrection, merited for us by Jesus. This group includes:

1. The Resurrection of Jesus from the Dead.
2. The Ascension of Jesus into Heaven.
3. The Descent of the Holy Spirit upon the Apostles.
4. The Assumption of Mary into Heaven.
5. The Coronation of Mary as Queen of Heaven.

Not all of the mysteries of the Rosary are mysteries properly speaking. But it is customary to call them such because they contain not only obvious but also more hidden, deeper lessons for the Christian life which need to be rediscovered and reabsorbed over and over, for more perfect imitation of Jesus and Mary.

In meditating on the Rosary we proceed as follows. We devote the first decade to meditating on the first mystery of a given group, the second decade to meditating on the second mystery, etc. As for which group of mysteries to use for a given Rosary, there is no hard and fast rule, at least in private recitation. One may choose the mysteries that have most immediate appeal or application. In public recitation it is generally best to follow the following schedule: say the joyful mysteries on Monday and Saturday (except during Lent) and the Sundays from Advent to Lent; pray the luminous mysteries on Thursday (except during Lent); say the sorrowful mysteries on Tuesday and Friday throughout the year, and every day from Ash Wednesday until Easter; pray the glorious mysteries on Wednesday (except during Lent), and the Sundays from Easter to Advent.

Importance of the Meditation

For the moment, we want simply to stress the importance of meditating on the mysteries. St. Louis-Marie Grignion de Montfort expresses it in forceful manner: "The Rosary without meditation on the sacred mysteries of our salvation would almost be like a body without the soul."

A body without the soul: a corpse!

Pope Leo XIII wrote: "What we contemplate (in the Rosary) is something most grand and most wonderful, the fundamental mysteries of Christianity."

These are strong words, which the Pope was to repeat more than once. More of that, too, in due course, after considering in the next chapter the historical formation of the Rosary.

Chapter 2

ORIGIN OF THE ROSARY

A LONG-STANDING tradition puts the origin of the Rosary in the 13th century and ascribes it to St. Dominic, thought to have been inspired by the Virgin Mary. Modern historians speak more guardedly. They see a gradual evolution to its present form.

Concerning the Our Father, some authors think that less literate monks, unable to read or recite the 150 psalms of the choir Office, were expected to say as many Our Fathers instead.

With regard to the Hail Mary, part of it, the words of the Archangel, formed a popular devotion as early as the 11th century. The faithful prayed them in honor of the joys of Mary. St. Peter Damian played a large role in fostering the devotion. A further development occurred toward the end of the 13th century, when people began to pray the words of the Archangel before statues of Mary. They knelt or genuflected and brought flower coronets, especially of roses. These coronets, or "chapeaux," are thought to account for the name chaplet, and the roses for the name Rosary.

Somewhat later, to the joys of Mary were added her sorrows and her glories.

Not until the 14th century did it become common practice to include Our Fathers with the Hail Marys, for reasons which are not clear. About the same time, as mentioned earlier, began the use of the second part of the Hail Mary: "Holy Mary, Mother of God. . . ."

What proved to be the definitive structure of the Rosary, or nearly so, dates from the 15th century, which also saw a remarkable growth in its use. Both developments, in structure and popularization, were principally the work of the Dominican, Alain of Roche. But this great apostle of the Rosary preached as historical certain facts which he knew only through his private revelations. Considering how important it is to treat such revelations with utmost caution, one can be excused for not taking as literal certain miracles which Alain attributes to St. Dominic.

Proponents of the Rosary

Still, the fact remains that Alain, a great Breton missionary, was convincing not only to the populace he evangelized but also to his fellow Dominicans. The result was enormous progress for the Rosary. The faithful had indeed honored, first the joys then the sorrows and glories of Mary but with devotion that was more affective than theological.

The Dominican preachers of the gospel were careful not to offend this simple, sincere piety. As disciples of St. Thomas they knew there was a place for sentiment, but in their hands the joys of Mary were brought into line with the mystery of the Incarnation; her sorrows were more clearly pointed toward the mystery of Redemption; her glorification became a symbol and expression of eschatological happiness, the coronation of all the blessed in the fulfilled kingdom.

Thanks to these Dominicans the Rosary, without ceasing to be a perfectly Marian devotion, assumed the character of a theocentric and theological prayer, solidly based on the gospel. By the same stroke, its spiritual dimensions swelled to infinity. Embodying both the human element and the divine, by God's grace it became a veritable mine which spiritual writers have worked ever since.

Perhaps the best known among such writers is St. Louis-Marie Grignion de Montfort. His work, *The Wonderful Secret of the Most Holy Rosary*, is a major contribution to Rosarian literature. For all its wordiness, it has stood the test of time. Cited at large are writers before him. In addition, the author brings his own insights to bear on the richness of the prayers recited and the benefits gained from meditating on the mysteries.

Popes, too, have championed this devotion. In the 19th century, the most notable in this respect was Leo XIII. The eminent Pope devoted no less than ten encyclicals to the subject. If we add his other pronouncements between 1883 and 1901, the number comes to twenty-three. More recent Popes, including Pope John Paul II and the present Pope Benedict XVI, also have urged devotion to the Rosary.

Despite these high approbations, the Rosary has had its detractors in every age. But then, what doctrinal teaching has not had them? Still, it remained for the years after the Second Vatican Council to bring us some of the most inordinate criticism and attempts to meddle with this proven devotion. In a time of change like ours, perhaps this should not surprise us.

If we have a true understanding of the Rosary, of its biblical and theological foundations and its immense spiritual benefits, we can keep a tranquil mind, detractors notwithstanding.

Chapter 3

BIBLICAL FOUNDATIONS OF THE ROSARY IN THE OLD TESTAMENT

ONE of the criticisms made of the Rosary by detractors is its newness, recentness, compared to older forms of prayer. Admittedly, given the historical context, one can scarcely imagine the ascetics of the Desert reciting Hail Marys as they went about their daily life. But the criticism rests on a partial and superficial view of the matter. The truth is that the fundamental inspiration of the Rosary is not of late origin but goes back to the New Testament and even further, to the Old.

Throughout the Bible, we cannot but be impressed by the constant calling to mind of God's interventions in the history of his People. Devout Israelites and the prophets refer to them again and again, either by way of simple *reminder* or to offer *motives* of supplication.

1. Remembrance of God's Wonderful Works

Whole psalms are devoted to this theme. Among them is Psalm 136, a liturgical litany called the "Great Hallel," which was recited in the Passover ritual after the "Little Hallel" (Psalms 113-118):

Give thanks to the Lord, for he is good,
    for his love endures forever. . . .

15

He alone does great wonders,
for his love endures forever.
In his wisdom he made the heavens,
for his love endures forever.

After the blessings of creation, there follows a long enumeration of God's interventions to bring the Hebrew people from Egypt into Canaan:

He struck down the firstborn of Egypt,
for his love endures forever, etc.

Psalm 105 particularizes even more:

Give thanks to the Lord, invoke his name;
proclaim his deeds among the peoples.
Offer him honor with songs of praise,
recount all his marvelous deeds.

And proclaimed they are: from the history of the patriarchs and Joseph, to Moses and the plagues of Egypt, followed by the Passover and the journey through the wilderness, and finally the entrance into Canaan, land promised to Abraham.

The following psalm, 106, is just as long and detailed, but from a different perspective. Reviewed is the Israelites' resistance to God's plan, in a psalm that amounts to a national confession of sinfulness.

Other psalms revive the theme of thankfulness, expressed in keeping God's law. Such is Psalm 78:

These things we have heard and know,
for our ancestors have related them to us,

We will not conceal them from our children;
  we will relate to the next generation,
  the glorious and powerful deeds of the Lord. . . .

In turn they were to tell their children,
  so that they would place their trust in God,
and never forget his works
  but keep his commandments.

The psalms, and sacred history generally, often sing God's praise for his creation, as in Psalm 104:

Bless the Lord, O my soul!
  O Lord, my God, you are indeed very great.
You are clothed in majesty and splendor,
  wrapped in light as in a robe.
You have stretched out the heavens like a tent;
  you have established your palace upon the
    waters.
You make the clouds serve as your chariot;
  you ride forth on the wings of the wind.
You appointed the winds as your messengers
  and flames of fire as your ministers, etc.

In a similar vein, Psalms 8, 103, 107, 135 and others; also Daniel 3:57ff.

Nor should the prophets be overlooked. How often they recall the wondrous deeds of God to arouse the faith and hope of their compatriots and exhort them to hold fast to the God of their fathers.

To conclude, we cite this oratorical passage from Deuteronomy:

Ask now about the days of old, the former times. From the day that God created humans upon the earth, inquire from one end of the heavens to the other, has anything so great ever happened or has anything like it been heard of? Has any other people heard the voice of God speak from the midst of the flame, as you heard, and still live? Did God ever go and lead one nation from the midst of another nation by trials, signs, wonders, and battle, with a mighty hand and an out-stretched arm, with great and wondrous deeds, all things that the LORD your God did for you in Egypt before your very eyes?

You were shown these things so that you might come to know that the LORD is God, there is no other besides him. (Deut 4:32-35).

2. Motives of Supplication

Combined with recall of the past is often an argument, or meditation, or some other mental operation which serves as basis for a particular request, individual or collective.

Such is Psalm 77:

I reflect on the days of old
  and recall the years long past.
At night I meditate in my heart,
  and I reflect, my spirit questions:

Will the Lord cast us off forever
  and never again show us his favor?
Has his kindness vanished forever?
  Has his promise ceased for all time?

Has God forgotten how to be merciful?
  Has he shut up his compassion in anger?

Or Psalm 143:

My spirit is faint within me,
  my heart has succumbed to fear.
I remember the days of old,
reflecting on all your actions,
  and meditating on the works of your hands.

Or again Psalm 44:

In God we boast the whole day long,
  and we praise your name forever.
But now you have rejected and humiliated us,
  and you no longer accompany our armies.
You forced us to retreat before the enemy;
  those who hate us plunder us unceasingly.

Awake! O Lord. Why do you sleep?
  Rise up, and do not abandon us forever.
Why do you hide your face
  and continue to ignore our misery and our suffer-
    ings?

The same emphases are found in the sages of Israel,
for example in Sirach (36):

Have pity on us, Master, Lord of the universe,
  and put the nations in dread of you.

Give new signs and work other wonders;
  show forth the glorious splendor of your right
    hand and arm.

Gather all the tribes of Jacob,
  and grant them their inheritance as you did in ear-
    lier times.

> Show mercy, Lord, to the people called by your
> name;
> Israel, whom you treated as your firstborn.

Examples of this kind could be multiplied, from the psalms, from the sages of Israel, and the prophets. Isaiah, for instance, at the very beginning says:

> Listen, O heavens, and pay close attention, O earth,
> for the Lord is speaking.
> I reared children and brought them up,
> but they have rebelled against me.
> An ox knows its owner
> and an donkey its master's stall,
> but Israel does not know,
> my people do not understand.

3. Cultic Memorial

We have seen that past events of Israel's history were an essential element in the spiritual life of devout Jews. They kept them alive, not only in thought and memory but by a sort of *reviviscence of the past in the present.*

This abiding presence was often made concrete by the ancient Hebrews through objects that became memorials in a very real sense: stones, mounds, steles (engraved slabs or pillars). See Gen 31: 45-54; Jos 4:6, 7, 9, etc.

But above all, it was in their liturgy, their official worship, that they relived the past most intensely, so much that they considered it as present. In so doing they were adhering to the instructions of their fathers, notably in Exodus and Deuteronomy.

For example, Ex 12:24-27:

"You shall observe this command as a fixed rite for yourselves and your children forever. When you will have entered into the land that the Lord will give you, as he promised, you shall observe this rite. When your children ask you, 'What does this rite of yours mean,' you shall tell them, 'It is the sacrifice of the Passover of the Lord, who passed over the houses of the children of Israel in Egypt when he struck the Egyptians and spared our houses.' "

And Deut 6:20-25:

"In the future when your son asks you, "What is the meaning of the decrees and statutes and ordinances that the Lord, our God, has commanded of you," you are to tell your son, "We were slaves to Pharaoh in Egypt, but the Lord brought us out of Egypt with a mighty hand. The Lord performed signs and wonders in our sight, great and terrible things, that he imposed upon Egypt and upon Pharaoh and upon all of his household. He brought us out from there so that he might bring us into and give to us the land that he promised to our fathers.

"The Lord commanded us to observe all of these statutes and to fear the Lord, our God, so that we might always prosper and be kept alive, even as we are today. If we are diligent in observing all of these commandments before the Lord, our God, as he commanded of us, then this will be our righteousness."

Today still, religious Jews who participate in their prescribed worship do not consider their past history as completely past but as having repercussions in the present.

Chapter 4

BIBLICAL FOUNDATIONS OF THE ROSARY IN THE NEW TESTAMENT

WITH the New Testament the theme changes. God's wondrous works are not those of temporal liberation for the Hebrew people, but those of spiritual liberation for humanity.

And the center is Jesus Christ.

It is he of whom the evangelists tell, and on whom the Apostles meditate.

It is he whom the first liturgical hymns acclaim, like the strophe of St. Paul which recalls three groups of mysteries in the Rosary:

Though he was in the form of God,
he did not regard equality with God
something to be grasped.

Rather, he emptied himself,
taking the form of a slave,
being born in human likeness.

Being found in appearance as a man,
he humbled himself,
and became obedient to death,
even death on a cross.

Because of this, God greatly exalted him
and bestowed on him the name
that is above all other names,

so that at the name of Jesus
every knee should bend
of those in heavens and on earth and under the
   earth,
and every tongue should proclaim
to the glory of God the Father:
JESUS CHRIST IS LORD!

Accordingly, it is the Christian revelation that guides us Christians as we contemplate the wonders in the life of Jesus, even as the ancient Jews contemplated the wonders of God's action in their history.

Moreover, it so happens that in the Mother of Jesus herself, the Virgin Mary, we have the most perfect model of this Christian contemplation.

Confidences of Mary

In the second chapter of St. Luke's Gospel there are two verses which look deceptively simple but in fact must be probed to be appreciated. In the Latin Vulgate they read as follows:

V. 19: *Maria autem conservabat omnia verba haec, confereris in corde suo.*

V. 51: *Et mater ejus conservabat omnia verba haec in corde suo.*

The first refers to the events experienced by Mary from the announcement of John the Baptist's birth to the birth of Jesus at Bethlehem. The second refers to events that followed, concluding with the finding of the Child Jesus in the Temple. Translators generally agree on the following reading:

V. 19: But Mary kept all these things (or, these memories), pondering them in her heart.

V. 51: And his mother kept all these things in her heart.

One point that seems beyond question is that these verses could only come from Mary, from her confi-dences, regardless of how St. Luke knew them, whether directly from Mary or through documents going back to Mary.

The hypothesis of confidences to Luke in person has much in its favor and is accepted by many. When the evangelist joined St. Paul on the Apostle's second missionary journey (Acts 16:11), he set down his recollections which later served him in writing the invaluable Acts of the Apostles. The year was 50, hence twenty years after the death of Jesus.

The Prologue of Acts (1:1) tells us that this work was preceded by another, the third Gospel, in preparation for which St. Luke made careful inquiry of events (Lk 1:1-4). These unquestionable texts support the conclusion that the evangelist had largely finished assembling the material for his Gospel twenty years after the death of Jesus. In all probability the Virgin Mary was still living at the time.

For the record we should mention that some exegetes, followers of Bultmann, place publication of the two works of St. Luke at a late date, later even than the destruction of Jerusalem (70 A.D.). This view is belied by the texts. There is not a word in the Acts of the Apostles to suggest that it was written after the destruction of Jerusalem. At the beginning of the present century Fillion himself remarked:

"Not only does it not give the least hint of this terrible event, but it speaks of the Temple, of worship, sacrifices, synagogues, in a word, of things Jewish as still existing as usual in the capital of Israel" (*La Sainte Bible*, VII, p. 607; Letouzey et Ané, Paris, 1901).

Moreover, there is no mention of St. Paul's martyrdom, which certainly took place before 70, probably in 67. Hence, we can be reasonably sure, according to St. Luke's own text, that the Acts of the Apostles was written well before 70. And since the author says that this work was preceded by his Gospel, we ought take his word for it. Very likely, then, St. Luke had written his Gospel when he joined St. Paul at Troas, which would place it before the year 50. From that time on, he could devote himself both to a fervent apostolate and to the scrupulous editing of the record of facts to which he was witness.

Because he hailed from Antioch, he was no doubt a convert from Greek paganism. But his commitment to write a Gospel and the book of Acts indicates that he was not a belated convert. There is even some reason to think, as some authors suggest, that he was the anonymous companion of Cleopas (Lk 24:13-35), so vivid and so personal is the account of what happened on the Emmaus road. And who knows but that he was not one of the 72 disciples (Lk 10:1), as has been conjectured?

In any case, it is a safe conclusion, supported by Pierre Pierrard and other biblical historians, that "Luke lived for a time in the company of Mary."

Corroboration: Hebraisms

Analysis of the verses in question confirms the association of Luke with Mary, because we find there two Hebraisms which the remarkable Hellenist that Luke was could not have introduced on his own.

The first is the word *verba*, which occurs in both verses. This Latin word is an exact translation of the Greek *rêmata*. The literal meaning of both is "words" (spoken). It is clear, however, that Mary remembered not only the words she heard but many things connected with them. How could St. Luke have been so imprecise? Simply because the Hebrew word itself used by the Virgin Mary (*dabar*, plural *debarim*) is imprecise, meaning both word and thing. The context decides the sense, and translators have not hesitated to write *things* (or memories) instead of *words*. St. Luke was aware of this characteristic of *dabar* and reflects it in his translation; for instead of *logos*, a more intellectual and abstract term, he chose *rêma*, which is more concrete though much less productive of derived meanings.

The second Hebraism is the word *heart*, also found in both verses. In the Hebrew this word has a much broader connotation than in French or English. It calls to mind not only what psychologists call affectivity but mental faculties in general: memory, judgment, reasoning. As we shall see more abundantly, it is in this Hebraic sense that Mary speaks of her heart.

In passing, a word should be said about the lightness, or ignorance, with which the "canticles" in the first two chapters of St. Luke's Gospel are sometimes dismissed as the evangelist's fabrication, pure and simple. These two verses, or what they reveal, help to expose such criticism. Like the verses, the canticles are marked by Hebraisms, far too many to be the work of a Hellenist.

Latent Meaning of the Two Verses

Another term piques curiosity, given in Latin as *conferens*. This translates the Greek participle *sumballousa*. The term is of considerable interest for our purpose. In the Greek we find the prefix *sun*, indicative of union, and the verb *ballô*, which means to "throw" or "hurl." Its first meaning, then, is to "throw together." But this is somewhat rare. More often it means to "place in common," to bring together, to join, hence the idea of comparing or confronting.

How should it be translated?

Most vernacular Bibles settle for "meditating, pondering." But one can meditate on an idea or event and scrutinize it without necessarily drawing parallels or comparisons. This is so true that commentators feel compelled to draw attention to it in a footnote.

For example, Pirot-Clamer: "She meditated on these things, compared the promise with the realization."

And Fillion: "Wonderful reflection, in which we can read the inmost heart of Mary. She compared what she saw and heard with the earlier revelations she had received, and she was in adoration of the wonders of the divine plan."

This says it all: she *saw* (the things) and *heard* (the words)—the two meanings of *dabar*—and she *com-*

pared all that with her own experience and with the wonders of the divine plan.

Searching Out the Hebrew Substrate

Modern biblical scholars look for Hebrew or Aramaic substrates in the writings of the New Testament, and their efforts have borne fruit in exegetical discoveries. The substrate of particular interest to our purpose has to do with the verb used by Mary in her vernacular tongue and rendered in the Greek of St. Luke by the participle *sumballousa.* What is the precise meaning of Mary's vernacular as revealed in the Semitic substrate of Luke's Greek? For an answer we consulted an eminent scholar, who sent a learned reply, in substance as follows:

First of all, he pointed out that the Semitic substrate of *sumballô* is not Aramaic, as used to be thought, "but since Qumran it is much more probable that the substrate was Hebrew."

He then looked into the Hebrew, and he cites not fewer than a dozen different opinions as to the root of the original verb. He himself thought that preference lay with the two Hebrew verbs HGH and SYH.[1] The first means to "murmur, repeat, say over and over," and the second means to "meditate, take an interest in, reflect on."

Scholar that he is, he would not make a choice, and the author is not in a position to do it for him. What we can propose is a tentative solution which may not be

---

1. Early Hebrew writing had only consonants. Vowels came later: hâgâh. . . .

scientific but has the advantage of being concordant with the discussion of the preceding chapter.

In other words, it seems to us that the two meanings of the two Hebrew verbs are found closely connected upon examination of the underlying mental activities:

1. When we are preoccupied with an idea, we keep coming back to it. We "murmur" it, "repeat" it to ourselves, "say it over and over." This is the Hebrew verb HGH.

2. Normally, we do not stop there, simply remembering the idea or holding it in mind. We naturally pass on to the next step of mental activity, the level of judgment and critique or evaluation. We "reflect on it, take an interest, meditate." Here we recognize the verb SYH.

A close look at verse 19 of St. Luke shows that it combines the two meanings.

1. With the verb *conservabat* (Mary kept these things), we are on the level of memory or holding in mind. And this is the meaning of the Hebrew HGH, even though a different Hebrew verb might express this meaning better.

2. With the participle *conferens* (meditating, pondering), we are more precisely in the realm of inventive and evaluative activity of the mind, as we saw in connection with the Greek *sumballô*. And this is the meaning of the Hebrew SYH.

All in all, then, it would seem that this verb SYH best corresponds to *conferens*.

But whichever verb we use, in Hebrew, Latin, or our vernaculars, it seems impossible to do justice to the Greek *sumballousa* without recourse to paraphrase. In the end it matters little. The harvest, in this case, can accommodate them all.

Before going on with our study we should point out something else our learned exegete made mention of, namely, that the Old Testament not infrequently associates the two Hebrew verbs HGH and SYH with the notion of heart in its Semitic sense (Ps 77:7; Is 33:18: Prov 15:28). Which is to say, it is one and the same intellectual and affective ambiance that permeates the Old Testament and the text of St. Luke.

More concretely, the Virgin Mary was in spiritual step with her ancestors in faith, whose spiritual walk also was characterized by remembrance of God's wondrous deeds, with a view to further blessings or to give him thanks.

Mary not only saw the end of the ancient order; in her began the new, the Messianic age. To the events she experienced she responded with the twofold activity of soul that characterized all religious Jews: she remembered *(conservabat)* and she considered in her heart *(conferens)*.

Spirituality of the New Testament

The aforesaid exegetical findings shed a good deal of light on the interior of Mary, not least the fact that she felt the need of repeating the same thing at such a short interval. In the two verses in question we find mostly identical terms: *conservabat, verba, corde.* Only the verbal *conferens* is distinctive of verse 19. But it is obvious that Mary's thoughts and feelings are the same in both instances. St. Luke's slight abridgment of verse 51 may have been a stylistic touch.

It is certain that Mary's spiritual life at this time was completely centered on contemplating and exploring the first mysteries of the Christian faith: Annunciation, Visitation, Nativity, Presentation, finding of the Child Jesus in the Temple.

She contemplated, i.e., she had the gift of contemplation. But she also strove for insight. In other words, she practiced *active prayer*. Spiritual writers point out that contemplative prayer properly speaking is a summit to which meditation is directed. True enough, just so we remember that infused (i.e., purely contemplative) prayer is a grace not given to everyone. And if at times we have it, the example of Mary, this model of perfect holiness, shows that it is compatible with active engagement of the mental faculties. Hence it is wise in principle to return to the labor of meditation, and attend on the fruits of contemplation, should it ensue. This, in essence, is what Mary does in her Magnificat. She speaks her personal reflections, along with an appreciation of the constant in God's interventions: a total liberty that holds no acceptance of persons or situations but considers only humility and the abandonment to Providence.

The Sorrowful and Glorious Mysteries

Scrutiny of the texts shows that the prayer life of Mary, during the first years of Christianity, was totally nourished by the mysteries we call joyful. She lingered over them in memory, and searched them in mind. It was her way of prayer.

Was there a change later on? A neglect or forgetfulness of subsequent mystery-events? How could there have been, for there is no doubt that she followed closely everything her Son did? No doubt, for example, that more than once in her life she thought of the miracle at the wedding of Cana, the more so that it was her intervention that brought about an alteration in the plans of her Son (luminous mystery). No doubt, either, that to her last moments on earth she recalled the sorrowful and glorious mysteries.

We know that she was at the foot of the cross (Jn 19:25). How could she have forgotten or neglected this moment of the world's salvation, or events that led up to it? We know that she was in the upstairs room on the day of Pentecost (Acts 1:14). How could the memory of such a wonder not have inspired her praise and thanksgiving, her prayers for the conversion of sinners, her desire to rejoin her Son in heaven?

In view of this, we can be sure that when we meditate on the twenty mysteries of the Rosary (and possibly on other episodes of the gospel), we are following exactly the method of prayer that was Mary's. Perhaps we do not match her in constant progress of prayer, or in the illuminations of heart and mind which she achieved. In addition, to judge from the experience of Christian mystics, there no doubt came a time when she would often find herself in deepest contemplation of God's works, without conscious mental effort on her part. But essentially her way of prayer was the same as ours.

We can also take it for granted that in heaven, where she sees all in God, Mary continues to give thanks for the "great things" the Lord wrought through her, on which she meditated in faith. And it is rightly conjectured that she has a predilection for Marian souls, who on earth continue to pray as she prayed.

Prayer Doubly Marian

The prayer life of Mary gives us a sense of the merits of the Rosary. Its technique is ancestral, with roots in methods of devotion going back before Christ, to the Old Testament. After the Incarnation of Christ the technique abides, and in the Rosary extends the authentic meditation of the holiest of Christians, the Virgin Mary. This alone qualifies it as a Marian prayer.

But there is more. In the Rosary we pray not only *like Mary*; we pray *through her*. It is in and through her that we view all the mysteries we meditate on, even those of which she may not have had firsthand knowledge. Our Hail Marys are most of all salutations addressed directly to Mary. And it is with her eyes, so to speak, and her heart that we enter into the mysteries of her Son, which also are hers. Hence the Rosary is a Marian prayer for a twofold reason: as *imitation* of Mary and *invocation of Mary*.

Mastering the technique of the Rosary, as distinct from mere nominal recitation, may take some time. Most individuals must lean on the imagination and the so-called "reconstitution of places," an aid to meditation well known in classical spirituality. In this regard, spiritual reading is especially helpful. It builds a store of "pictures" and recollections for praying the Rosary. On the other hand, people of a more intellectual bent feel less need of the imagination. Not that they are exempt from spiritual reading, but when they pray the Rosary, simple recall of a mystery suffices.

The important thing in all this is to conform to one's temperament. In any case, however, nothing will be gained without effort. But the results are more than worth the price, especially if the effort is sustained.

We shall come back to this point in Chapter 12.

Chapter 5

THE ROSARY: CHRISTIAN PRAYER

MUCH talked about today are Oriental methods of prayer, especially zen and yoga. Some authors, convinced that they can be "baptized" and made part of Christian practice, actively promote them by word and deed, at organized conferences and in publications. Others, as well informed if not better, see a snare. In their view the essential of these methods cannot be assimilated by Christianity.

Actually, both sides in this debate have a point, depending on how the issue is defined.

1. If zen, yoga, and other Oriental methods are taken to mean nothing more than their *physiological and psychological techniques*, there seems no reason why they cannot be used in Christianity. They are a kind of bodily and mental gymnastics, which may be helpful to persons who cannot get their daily cares out of mind and need a crutch to collect themselves and fix attention.

At the same time, it should be noted that thousands of Christian mystics and ascetics have been the glory of Christianity, from the beginning to the present, without having to wait on these techniques to produce the same results.

2. If, however, one proposes to go all the way with these techniques, seeking the *mental void* preached

by gurus and other Oriental masters, it is clear that this is incompatible with prayer such as we have shown it practiced by the sages of the Old Testament and the Virgin Mary. For us, Christians, the ideal is not an intellectual void, emptiness attended by some vague grasp of the Absolute. Our ideal is fullness, fullness of contemplation as we behold the wonders of God's plan for humanity through four thousand years, and especially the wonder of his plan in the Incarnation of his Son.

These manifestations of our God do not leave us to our own devices, nor have for their promise a distant, often pantheistic, hold of the Divine. Rather, they wrench us out of our egoisms so as to be plunged in the heart of transcendent Deity. With that, we are at opposite extremes to the end sought by Oriental methods, and in the domain of sanctifying grace.

More could be said on this subject.[1] Suffice some remarks by an author who has been director of the Ricci Institute in Taiwan and professor of the history of religions in Manila, Father Yves Raguin. He has also produced a Sino-European dictionary. We cite from his work, *L'Attention au mystère (Attention to Mystery)* (Desclée de Brouwer, 1979), whose content was first delivered in Chinese to Chinese students:

"The purpose of these methods (he writes) is to provide means of developing the self in its deepest capacities. Their aim is improvement of the human self and development of its latent potentialities. . . .

---

1. For additional comments by the author, see *l'Ami du Clergé,* Feb. 16, 1966 and Sept. 13, 1973, reviewing two books by Father Lassale.

"These methods of gaining mastery of the mind and becoming aware of its ulterior capacities are as old as the world, but they have been especially developed in India through yoga, and in China and Japan with zen. Confucianism also has developed methods of cultivating the self which have nothing to do with religious striving. Likewise, Taoism has developed very elaborate methods intended to foster the vital energies of the self, etc." (pp. 18-19).

The point is well made. According to Father Raguin neither yoga, nor zen, nor Taoism, nor other methods of China, Japan or India are essentially religious in nature: "their aim is improvement of the human self," a sort of physical or intellectual culture. In the Christian scheme of things it is God whom we seek, God with whom we are united through the love and contemplation resulting from infused grace.

Christian Methods

It could be very dangerous to embrace Oriental methods indiscriminately. There is the risk to let slip the historical plan of Revelation, i.e., the temptation of trying to meditate on a sort of nontemporal level in which concrete, historical realities of the Incarnation are disdained and disregarded.

This danger is not imaginary. Some priests have become so orientalized as to preach access to God without passing through the sacred Humanity of Jesus. The tendency is not new, having cropped up at various times in Christianity. But it is rejected in the strongest terms by St. Paul, by St. John, and by all Doctors and saints faithful to the magisterium of the Church.

People who pray the Rosary with faith and devotion run no danger. This prayer is centered on Jesus Christ, Son of God and Son of Mary. Of its very nature it leads to God, but through Jesus Christ and in Jesus Christ.

Moreover, the continual recourse to Mary as we meditate on the mysteries accentuates the atmosphere of loving-kindness that speaks of God's boundless mercy toward his sinful creatures.

In such conditions there is nothing to lead to doctrinal error or contemplation tinged with pride and self-assertion.

Chapter 6

THE ROSARY: SCHOOL OF PRAYER

AT the beginning of his *Confessions* St. Augustine writes: "You have made us for yourself, O Lord, and our hearts are restless till they rest in you." This is the experience of all who thirst for the Absolute. It is what makes them seek out deserts, knock on the door of cloisters, and cross oceans. They have learned that happiness is found only in God, and are prepared to renounce everything in order to live for him alone.

But how many people are in a position to leave everything and devote themselves exclusively to God? Most men and women are bound by a state of life that precludes this choice. Is the spiritual life denied to them?

Not at all. Saints of great understanding, like St. Francis de Sales, spent time and talent to show that it is possible to live a holy life in the world. Many books on spirituality have been written to this end, especially in modern times. Reading them is always profitable.

Among the secrets of the spiritual life, one of the most effective is without a doubt recitation of the Rosary. Bishop d'Hulst wrote in his letters of spiritual direction: "I have known ordinary people of little education who prayed the Rosary in sublime fashion." How so? Because, he explains, the Rosary is "an easy initiation to contemplation of *mysteries* which show us the *living God* in action."

Theological Prayer

The Rosary is in fact a very simple yet very sure way of arriving at contemplation. To see this we have only to consider the traditional degrees of mental prayer, which are clearly described, for example, in Father Lemonnyer's work *Our Divine Life.*

The first level of mental prayer is *meditation.* Here the considerations are mostly moral. Attention revolves around such matters as life and death, virtues and vices, motives for leading a good life, etc.

A more advanced level is *theological,* which is characterized by activity of the infused virtues of faith, hope, and divine charity. In theological prayer the soul habitually turns to God in expressions of adoration, love, thanksgiving, self-surrender, and in a word actively pursues all the resources of our supernatural life.

Having progressed this far, there remains only one step for the soul to reach the summit, which is passive *mystical prayer,* fruit of the gifts of the Holy Spirit.

The Rosary is an excellent instrument of sanctification at all three levels. We shall speak later of its moral effects. With regard to its role as a theological prayer— its effect on faith, hope, and divine charity—this has been attested by the highest authorities.

The Rosary Deepens Faith

Concerning *faith,* there are many references in Leo XIII. For example, in his Encyclical of Sept. 7, 1892:

"Among persons, families, and whole nations where the practice of the Rosary is honored, we need not fear that ignorance or pernicious error will destroy the faith."

Similarly, Pius XI:

"Above all, the Rosary nourishes the Catholic faith, which grows stronger by meditation on the sacred mysteries and elevates the mind to truths revealed by God."

In his *Wonderful Secret of the Most Holy Rosary* St. Louis-Marie Grignion de Montfort had said:

"Never will a soul that prays the Rosary every day become a formal heretic or be deceived by the devil. This is a proposition that I would seal with my blood."

Time has borne him out. Thanks to the Rosary the Japanese Christians of Urukami persevered in the faith despite persecutions. Thanks to the Rosary the Vendean Catholics of France held fast in the upheaval of the Revolution. And the reason that the Catholics of Tonkin (now part of Vietnam) persevered and increased was because the Spanish missionaries who came to preach the gospel to them at the end of the 19th century were Dominicans who understood the importance of introducing them to the Rosary. The Tonkinese remained faithful to the Rosary, prayed it in their homes, wore it around the neck, and made it the basis of their devotional life.

It is not hard to see that the Rosary nourishes our faith. In the joyful mysteries it has us meditate on the wonders of the Incarnation. In the luminous mysteries we recall the ministry of Christ. In the sorrowful mysteries it re-creates the phases of the Lord's Passion, culminating in the redemption of the world. And in the glorious mysteries it points to the foundation of supernatural faith: God as rewarder (Heb 11:6).

The Rosary Fosters Hope

Hope also is fostered in the mysteries of the Rosary.

The Incarnation (joyful mysteries) is the fulfillment of the great messianic hope. Thus, the aged Simeon, as he held in his arms the Child Jesus, hope of the world, could say his beautiful prayer known as the *"Nunc Dimittis"*:

"Now, Lord, you may dismiss your servant in peace, according to your word;
for my eyes have seen your salvation,
which you have prepared in the sight of all the peoples,
a light of revelation to the Gentiles
and glory for your people Israel" (Lk 2:29-32).

The Passion (sorrowful mysteries) was the price of our Redemption and gives us hope in God despite our past sins. The saintly Sister Mary Martha Chambon was taught by our Lord to pray as follows: "Eternal Father, I offer you the wounds of our Lord Jesus Christ as healing for the wounds of our souls." This prayer is an affirmation of the unfailing remedy we have against despair in the merits of Jesus.

So, too, the glorious mysteries confirm the aspirations of the Christian, the hope for heaven and the glories we are promised.

In an encyclical on the Rosary which we cited earlier Pius XI said:

"The Rosary enlivens the hope for the things above that endure forever. As we meditate on the glory of Jesus Christ and his Mother, we see heaven opened, and are heartened in our striving to gain the eternal home."

The Rosary Increases Love

Concerning love, the divine *charity*, Pius XI said in the same place:

"How could it not but be made more fervent by the Rosary? We meditate on the suffering and death of our Redeemer and the sorrows of his afflicted Mother. Will we not make a return of love for the love received?"

Meditating on the Passion of Jesus is an infallible means of stirring up our love for him. On this score, let no one cry "dolorism." Concentration on the suffering Jesus is simple acknowledgment of a reality. That is why so many saints, in the Middle Ages in particular but also to this day, have made it the center of their devotional life.

Devotion to the other mysteries works to the same effect, stirring up the soul to love. St. Bernard, St. Theresa of the Child Jesus, and many others increased their love by thus contemplating the Child Jesus. And St. Paul, while preaching a "Christ crucified" (1 Cor 1:23 and 2:2), spoke of his Glory in unsurpassable terms.

Contemplative Prayer

But is there also, properly speaking, a contemplative value to the Rosary? Pope Paul VI did not hesitate to use the word. Recommending the Rosary, Oct. 8, 1969, he noted that through meditation on the mysteries of Christ in union with his blessed Mother, "the prayer of petition is transformed, so to speak, into contemplative prayer."

Three principal reasons for this may be cited:

1. The succession of events and persons in the Rosary favors a *global view of the Truth* presented.

What does a mountain climber who has reached the top have in common with the patron of an art gallery who is fascinated by the beauty of a painting? Both are afforded a global view of an harmonious whole, enhanced by a multitude of imperceptible touches which contribute to the general impression. This is natural contemplation.

Something like this happens in supernatural contemplation, especially in the contemplation of the mysteries of the Rosary. On the pictorial level, for example, popular custom associates the joyful mysteries with white roses, the sorrowful with red roses, and the glorious with golden roses and more recently purple or blue flowers have been suggested to represent the luminous mysteries. In other words popular piety has always sensed an underlying kinship among the mysteries of each group. This is the global view, the contemplative view.

There is also an analytic moment, when we pass from one mystery to another. Here again, there is contemplation, though of short duration. The relatively rapid succession of mysteries sustains attention and fosters the contemplative view of the whole group.

2. This contemplation is fostered even more because the events meditated on in the Rosary are both simple and *profound.*

They are simple, because they are lived events, perceptible, and tangible. They are not philosophical or theological abstractions. To understand them, there is no need of higher learning; the catechism will do. A child can grasp them as well as—and perhaps better than—an adult. They are within reach of anyone.

At the same time, they are so profound that no knowledge, acquired or infused, will ever exhaust them. The longer and more lovingly we view them, the more their horizon opens and their richness unveils. Hence, we can come back to them repeatedly with joy undiminished and ever greater possibilities of contemplation.

3. Finally, the Rosary recited aloud leads to contemplation by reason of the *recitation in common.*

It is a fact now again admitted—after having been questioned for some time—that religious who take part in a dignified choir Office, in a devout and recollected manner, find it a stimulus to contemplative prayer. Even visitors who attend this chanting of psalms experience a spell of fervor and collectedness that borders on contemplation.

The same thing can be said of a Rosary recited in common, when one group alternates with another in praying the decades. The alternation permits continual shifting from vocal activity to comparative rest. If the Hail Marys are said in an edifying manner, with faith and devotion, those who say them are moved to contemplative recollection, and those who listen are similarly inspired.

As Lacordaire pointed out: "The rationalist smiles in contempt when he sees long lines of people filing by and saying the same thing over and over. More perceptive minds appreciate that love has only one word, and in saying that word over and over it never repeats itself."

Chapter 7

THE ROSARY:
SCHOOL OF MORAL FORMATION

TRADITIONALLY, among some people, recitation of the Rosary includes mention of a special "fruit" for each mystery. So, for the Annunciation: "fruit of the mystery, humility"; for the Visitation: "fruit of the mystery, charity," etc.

This alone is an indication of the moral value in meditating on the mysteries of the Rosary. But it is only part of the picture.

First, no single virtue can exhaust the moral productiveness of any mystery of the Rosary. For example, the mystery of the Annunciation is an endless source of inspiration not only for dogma but for the moral life as well: inspirations of faith, obedience, yielding to God, generosity, purity, etc.

And then, in order to do full justice to the Rosary's power of moral formation, account must also be taken of the general principles that govern moral activity.

In the main, these principles are three: motive power of images, the appeal of heroes, moral balance of real models.

1. Motive Power of Images

This power is a principle acknowledged by all psychologists. Every image naturally tends to produce a physiological reaction, a movement of some sort, however slight. Hence, the greater the obsession of an image or idea, the more likely it is to lead to action. Many suicides can be explained by the dominating power of the "fixed idea." On the positive side, healthy fixation on a high ideal stimulates the practice of virtue. Bossuet writes of this in his *Elevations (Discourses) on the Mysteries:*

"To counteract the wayward imagination, we must supply it with good images. When our memory is filled with them, it will reproduce only these devout images. A water wheel keeps turning, but it lifts only the kind of water found in the river. If the water is pure, the wheel lifts pure water; if it is impure, that is lifted. So, if our memory is filled with pure ideas, it has pure ideas to draw from and pure thoughts to suggest.

"A mill keeps grinding, but it grinds only what is put in. If it is barley, we have ground barley; if it is wheat, we have flour.

"Store the memory with pure and holy images, and then the imagination, at least ordinarily, will bring to mind only what is fine and pure."

These thoughts of Bossuet apply to the Rosary. If we recite it faithfully, day by day, we derive great moral benefit. The examples of virtue meditated on penetrate the subconscious, work on its deepest tendencies, and create a spiritual environment of purity and rectitude which enables us to overcome the attractions of the world and persevere in our moral effort. Leo XIII spoke of this as follows:

"We meditate on most excellent examples of modesty and humility, of patience in work, of goodwill toward our neighbor, of perfect performance of daily tasks, in short, examples of every virtue which cannot but become fixed in the memory and produce a change for the better in our daily thoughts and habits" (Encyclical of September 8, 1893).

2. "Appeal of Heroes"

The French philosopher Henri Bergson once remarked that the practice of virtue is promoted by the example of great men and women far more than by oratory. He called this attraction the "appeal of heroes."

In like manner but with greater reason we can also speak of the appeal of saints, heroes of a different sort with an influence all their own.

Conversions resulting from the example of saints are countless, from the first years of Christianity to the present time. Recall, by way of illustration, the Fathers of the Desert, all the conversions they inspired. And the conversion of St. Augustine, which he attributed in no small measure to the example of his saintly mother. Or a more recent saint, the Curé of Ars, who made the lives of the saints his daily reading.

In the mysteries of the Rosary there is still more, by far, than in the lives of the saints. The examples of Jesus are those of a God-Man. And the examples of the Virgin Mary shine with incomparable perfection. Jesus and his blessed Mother attract us both in their joys and in their sorrows.

In the words of Pope Leo XIII, found in the encyclical previously cited, the threefold division of the mysteries of the Rosary contains the remedy for the three great evils of our era: "aversion for the ordinary and everyday life of toil; unreasonable fear of all that causes pain and suffering; and indifference toward the afterlife."

3. Moral Balance

The threefold division of the mysteries of the Rosary also makes for balance in our moral life.

If, for example, we confined our meditation to the joyful events surrounding the infancy of Jesus, we would get an incomplete view of the reality. Certainly, one can have a preference for these mysteries, and the Church was not opposed to the founding of two contemplative orders by name of Sisters of the Annunciation. But with these Sisters an integral liturgical life guards against exclusiveness and leaves place for the sorrowful and glorious mysteries.

Similarly, those who would limit their horizon to the *Passion* of our Lord run the risk of having a defective morality, tending to "dolorism," far too austere and demanding. Here again, preference is permissible, since the dogma of the Redemption is central to our salvation and the history of Christian spirituality, especially in the Middle Ages, offers many examples of stigmatic saints whose influence was enormous.

However, these were special cases, where the grace of God providentially forestalled possible harm from such emphasis. Without this exceptional help even the best-intentioned souls are apt to go astray.

As for religious orders centered on the Passion (Servites, Passionists, etc.), for them as for others the liturgy redresses the balance.

Meditating on the *glorious* Christ without reference to his mortal life can lead to morality that is, so to speak, disembodied, removed from the material world and its burdens.

In the Rosary there is nothing to invite such dangers. In fact, it would be hard to find another prayer in which there is such perfect blending of all our tendencies, human and supernatural. This property of the Rosary, its equilibrium as regards the Christian life, has been noted by the Popes, for example, by Pius XII in the Encyclical *Ingruentium Malorum* of 1951:

"Through frequent meditation on the mysteries the soul inclines to, and grows in, the virtues they contain. It is filled with hope for the everlasting rewards and feels itself prodded, gently yet firmly, to follow the way of Christ and his Mother."

To conclude, the assiduous recitation of the Rosary is a powerful factor for moral progress, if we apply ourselves to it with goodwill and let the grace of God work in our souls.

Chapter 8

THE ROSARY: SCHOOL OF HOLINESS

IN view of what already has been said, the title of this chapter goes without saying. Profoundly Christian, the Rosary promotes a life of prayer and fosters the moral virtues. For this reason, to say no more, it is indeed a school of holiness.

In his work, *On the Trinity* (4, 28), St. Augustine writes: "To the extent that our spiritual life is in contact with an eternal reality, we are not in this world; and the souls of the righteous, even though still in the flesh, are not of this world according as they delight in divine realities."

This is what we do in the Rosary. We "delight in divine realities," which lifts us above the attractions of the material world and helps us to live on a saintly level. The more we attend to these realities in order to shape our life by them, the greater our progress in holiness.

But there is a way of praying the Rosary which is particularly helpful in making one's daily life more spiritually productive. What this is will become clear in a moment.

The Daily Rosary

Many people pray one decade daily. This is a good beginning, especially if it is done in collaboration with a group which taken together, prays the complete Rosary of twenty decades each day (as in the "Living Rosary").

Others pray five decades daily. This is the more frequent practice among devout souls.

A very small number pray the complete Rosary (twenty decades) on a daily basis, usually in four separate periods of the day, whenever they find the 20 minutes or so it takes for five decades. This is an excellent practice but not easy to maintain. As St. Thèrése of Lisieux remarked, it requires great effort when one is alone.

Without a doubt, the ideal way alluded to above, the one that yields the best spiritual results, is to begin the Rosary in the morning and then take advantage of opportune moments for continuing it throughout the day, mystery after mystery, all twenty. We could begin with the first decade on waking and while yet in bed. The mystery of the Incarnation would project its joyful mood on hours to come and dispel the drowsiness and weariness of these first minutes of the day.

Next, we could continue saying Hail Marys as we go about our usual tasks. Most often, the thoughts that flit in and out of mind during routine activities are perfectly useless. Much more profitable is to fill such times with invocations to Mary in the succession of mysteries, joyful, sorrowful, luminous, and glorious.

Some might say that praying under such conditions is fraught with distractions. That is true, but it is better than not praying at all.

The more so because what counts is not so much the materiality of the words that are said but the atmosphere of faith induced by saying them. The thought of going from one mystery to another keeps alive the spirit of contemplation, which transforms the most menial tasks into priceless pearls of eternity.

Consequently, when we pray according to this plan we are never wasting time but are always, so to speak, in a state of prayer. And that is preferable to spending a half hour on one's knees in the morning, and then forgetting about prayer the rest of the day.

Fosters the Practice of Constant Prayer

People who pray the Rosary in this manner are always surprised to find their days completely changed. The joyful mysteries brighten the morning hours. The "burden of the day and the scorching heat" are made more bearable by meditating on the luminous and sorrowful mysteries. And day draws to a close pervaded by a reflective presence of the glories to come.

According to the masters of the spiritual life, the practice of constant prayer—or maintaining a state of prayer—is an essential characteristic of holiness. It is an indispensable means for the soul to become absorbed in God so that all its thoughts, its decisions, and its activities reflect and manifest its life in God.

This is what St. Augustine had in mind when he said: "The soul that knows how to pray right knows how to live right." These words were a favorite of Blessed Augustine Kazotic, Dominican bishop and disciple of St. Thomas Aquinas. He, like other saints and blessed, practiced them to the point of spending whole nights in prayer, sometimes two or three consecutively, as recalled in the biographical sketch for the day of his feast (August 3).

Not everybody can do this. But it is a fact that today, no doubt in reaction to a materialist civilization, many young people aspire after a life of prayer as continual as possible.

To this extent, at least, and perhaps without realizing it, they typify the gospel, the Apostle Paul, and the first Christians.

Praying Always

In introducing the parable of the corrupt judge St. Luke indicates that its purpose was to teach the "necessity of praying always and not losing heart" (18:1).

There is reason to believe that Jesus himself did not actually state this purpose in so many words, but that Luke was simply referring to a common teaching of our Lord, of which the parable was an illustration. Jesus, for example, makes the same point in Lk 21:36: "So be on the watch. Pray constantly. . . ."

This is also a prominent theme in St. Paul's teaching. We could list many Pauline texts relating to constant prayer (Rom 1:10; 12:12; Eph 6:18; Col 1:3; 1 Thes 5:17; 2 Thes 1:11, etc.) and others conveying the idea of perseverance (2 Cor 4:1, 16; Gal 6:9; Eph 3:13; 2 Thes 3:13).

The first Christians took this teaching literally. The *Fathers of the Desert* in particular held to it. For example, St. Nilus:

"Just as breathing never stops, so should we address to God, until our final breath, the petitions of the heart."

And St. Evagrius:

"Whoever loves God is always speaking with him as with a father, laying aside every foolish thought.

"Prayer is the activity that becomes the intellect, its best and sufficient use.

"Just as sight is the most precious sense, so prayer is more divine than all the virtues."

It is by prayer, says Mother Syncletica, that we dispel "this senseless malaise which goes by the name of ennui (in Latin *acedia*, great enemy of the solitary). Frequent praying of psalms drives it out."

Apothegms on Praying Always

The *Apothegms* (sayings) of the Fathers of the desert in the 4th and 5th century insist on continual prayer:

"The true monk ought always have prayer and psalm-singing in his heart."

"The measure of prayer for a monk is to pray without measure."

"If a monk prays only when he is standing for prayer, that monk does not pray at all."

"Prayer consists in being in prayer not only at a certain time, but at all times."

"Whether you eat or drink, are on a walk or at work, never turn from prayer."

A Time-Tested Invocation

To help this purpose along the same Fathers advised against protracted conversation and recommended untiring repetition of the well-known verse "Deign, O God, to rescue me; O Lord, make haste to help me." In his famous *Conferences* John Cassian tells of this prayer and its indebtedness to the monachism of the desert:

"This is for your instruction, this formula of prayer that you are seeking. Every monk who looks for continual recollection of God uses it for meditation, and with the object of driving every other sort of thought from his heart. You cannot keep the formula before you unless you are free from all bodily care.

"The formula was given us by a few of the oldest fathers who remained. They did not communicate it except to a very few who were athirst for the true way. To maintain an unceasing recollection of God it is to be ever set before you. The formula is: 'Deign, O God, to rescue me; O Lord, make haste to help me (Ps 70:2).' This verse has rightly been selected from the whole Bible for this purpose. It fits every mood and temper of human nature, every temptation, every circumstance."

Cassian goes on to say that the verse "is an impregnable bulwark, a shield and coat of mail which no spear can pierce," no matter the vicissitudes of spiritual life, which are spelled out.

Use of Invocations

A closer examination of this practice might lead to the objection that the role of grace is not sufficiently safeguarded therein. Whatever the case, *other similar prayers* have been suggested throughout the centuries by various families of monks and religious.

St. Benedict, after speaking of the degrees of humility, encourages the use of a short invocation. St. Louis-Marie Grignion de Montfort recommends a brief consecration to Mary. And so on to the present day, when indulgences have been attached to various invocations, especially to the Sacred Heart and the Immaculate Heart of Mary, to encourage their use.

However, among all these short prayers, one has been particularly popular.

The Jesus Prayer

"Lord Jesus Christ, Son of God, be merciful to me, a sinner." This is the so-called Jesus Prayer, a condensation of two prayers in the Gospel, that of the man born blind and that of the publican (tax collector).

One of the first to mention it is Diadochus, a fifth-century bishop of Photice. In subsequent centuries John Climacus and, even more, Hesychius of Batos made it the basis of an entire spirituality. In the 13th and 14th century the monks of Mount Athos, largely through the enduring influence of St. Gregory of Sinai, experienced a renewal of fervor and began to pray this prayer to the accompaniment of bodily tactics: special postures and breath control.

In 1782 appeared the *Philocalia*, the work of Nicodemus the Hagiorite and Macanus of Corinth. It is an anthology on the interior life from the Fathers of the Desert. The Jesus Prayer is strongly recommended: "When you say it, let it be with all your will, with all your strength, with all your heart." Promised with it are sustained fervor and peace of soul.

Russian spiritual masters, particularly of the 19th century, attached much less importance to the bodily exercises. This simplification may explain why the popularity of the Jesus Prayer in Orthodox circles extended to the laity.

In time, it also caught on in the West, especially among Anglicans. And, for some years now, Catholics themselves have more and more taken to it. There are, in fact, sessions offered for its introduction, similar to those offered for zen and yoga.

What is one to make of it all?

Evaluation

A prayer that has proved itself for fifteen centuries commands our esteem. Among other things the Jesus Prayer has in its favor that, brevity notwithstanding, it is both dogmatic and moral.

Dogmatic: it professes our belief in the divinity of Jesus. He, the Son of God made man, is the one who saved us. So it is normal that our spiritual life be centered on him.

Moral: By the words "be merciful to me, a sinner," it both exemplifies and instills a deeply Christian attitude, comprising humility, repentance, and trust.

These two aspects, one moral and the other dogmatic, bring us to the heart of Christianity and invite us to search the abyss of its twofold mystery: that of Christ and that of our sinfulness.

In addition, because of its brevity it can be used in all circumstances and stresses of life, especially as it may be reduced to one word, the name of Jesus.

All in all, then, there is no reason why those who find this prayer helpful in their spiritual life should not only be devoted to it but also recommend it to others, ever mindful, however, of the wise counsel from a monk of the Eastern Church:

"Avoid imprudent zeal, all intemperate propaganda. Do not succumb to mistaken fervor, trumpeting this prayer as the best, still more, as the only one. The secrets of the King are not cried to the housetops."

Superiority of the Rosary

The Rosary, meditated on as we have suggested, is a means of being in constant prayer and has the advantage over other prayers, even the Jesus Prayer, for several reasons.

1. The Rosary Is More Self-forgetting

The Jesus Prayer, strictly speaking, is *individualistic*. We pray for ourselves: *be merciful to me*. This is good, and in line with forms of prayer that prevailed for centuries, the 19th century included. But our age prefers a broader outlook—indeed a universal one.

This is a gain. While it is proper and necessary to pray for oneself, it is also proper and even necessary to reach out to the larger world, indeed to all the world, as did Jesus and Mary in their redemptive action. The Rosary facilitates this *transition to the universal* through contemplation of the mysteries and meditation on their "spiritual fruits."

Devotees of the Jesus Prayer claim that it does not prevent them from extending their solicitude to the whole world. We believe them. It proves that they are not slaves to formulas. But a literal comparison leaves no doubt: priority goes to the Rosary.

2. The Rosary Enlarges the Horizon of Faith

It is true that in Jesus, Son of God made man, we have everything. Calling upon his Name, in persevering faith, is a sure means of salvation. But the Rosary, in detailing the various aspects of the person and the life of Jesus, enriches and enlarges our perceptions of the faith far more than the simple Jesus Prayer, or any similar invocation.

Some may contend that repetition of the Jesus Prayer makes us penetrate ever more deeply into the mystery of Christ. This is a valid contention. But it ought also to be acknowledged that this progress in spiritual insight is more effectively secured through meditation on the successive mysteries of the Rosary. This potential of the Rosary has been singled out many times by the Popes, especially by Leo XIII and John Paul II.

3. The Rosary Facilitates Contemplation by Its Variety

This third reason is similar to the preceding one, but the point of view differs. It speaks, not precisely of the object, the content, of faith but of faith in its bearing on activity of the mind.

Because of its sobriety the Jesus Prayer is more apt to become monotonous. Continual self-discipline is required in order to persevere in it from year to year, till the end of life. By contrast, the variety in the mysteries of the Rosary facilitates enormously the effort of contemplation.

4. The Rosary Is More Favorable to the Fulfillment of the Person

This last reason is the culmination of the others. It is generally admitted that there is an element of austerity, or spiritual leanness, to the Jesus Prayer which is overcome only after long years of practice.

In the Rosary, it is different. Effort is rewarded much sooner, in profusion. Intimate union with the Virgin Mary, the lesson ever new of each mystery, the charm of the joyful mysteries, the tragic mood of the sorrowful mysteries, the attraction of the luminous and glorious mysteries, all this and more expands the soul, rejoices it, elates it, enriches it, and fills it with spiritual good.

With these reasons, to which others could be added, we begin to see why the Blessed Virgin in her apparitions makes such earnest request of the Rosary and never mentions the Jesus Prayer. She knows that for the vast majority of souls the Rosary is the obvious choice.

Not that the two are incompatible, far from it. We can use them together, alternatively, reserving the Jesus Prayer (and similar invocations) for moments that do not permit recitation even of one Hail Mary. But it is clearly more in conformity with the intentions of the Virgin Mary to give preference to her Rosary, as a regular thing.

Examples of the Saints

Some people may feel that the Rosary is not for them, especially not a Rosary every day. Let them take heart and example not only from saintly priests and saintly religious but from men and women in the world who prayed the Rosary every day and found it an unfailing blessing in their life.

St. Teresa of Avila never went to bed without having said her Rosary, however late the hour.

St. Margaret Mary, recalling her childhood, said:

"I prayed to the most Blessed Virgin in all my needs, and she saved me from great dangers. I did not dare address her Son directly, but always went to her. My little garland to her was the Rosary, which I prayed kneeling on the ground, or making as many genuflections as there are Hail Marys, or kissing the ground as many times."

And, being a Sister at Paray-le-Monial, she prayed the Rosary every day, with fervor.

As she lay dying a young Spanish boy decided he would begin to pray three Rosaries daily. It was John Macias, who became one of the great Dominicans of Lima.

St. Louis-Marie Grignion de Montfort was not only devoted to the Rosary; he was also its indefatigable apostle, to the point that he would not set foot in a parish where it was neglected. He composed verses which became for him a means, not always artistic but always useful, for a renewal of fervor. An example is given by these stanzas concerning the Hail Mary:

Rising or going to bed,
Leaving or returning,
Away or at home,
I have it always on my lips.
I am insuperable
When I say my Hail Mary.
I am fully alive,
Fearing nought from the devil.

Salutary counsel,
Wonderful secret:
To become perfect,
Say a Rosary a day.

And, in the same vein, speaking of the Virgin Mary:

I pray to her constantly,
and imitate her everywhere.

This great saint has had a recent emulator in the person of the celebrated *Padre Pio*. Less occupied than St. Louis-Marie, he could tell his beads more assiduously. He had them in his hands day and night. When one Rosary was finished, he began another and sometimes said as many as a dozen in twenty-four hours.

Such was also the practice of another great apostle of Jesus and Mary, *Father Mateo*. During his two years of constant preaching in the Far East he told the missionaries that his only private prayer was the Rosary.

This recalls a similar confession of St. Francis de Sales. It is known that he made a vow to recite the complete Rosary (fifteen decades) every day. What is perhaps not so well known is something he said in confidence to St. Vincent de Paul, that "if he did not have the obligation of the Divine Office, he would say no other prayer than the Rosary." Could this have been the inspiration for a contemporary Congregation in India which has no other prayer Office than the Rosary?

Examples of Holy Priests

Another apostle of the Rosary was *Father Bellanger*, a French military chaplain at the end of the last century. He never hesitated to bring his soldiers around to say it. One of them detested guard duty. His attitude changed completely as a result of the Rosary: "My rifle in one hand, my Rosary in the other, the hours are short."

Father Charles de Foucauld, Trappist-hermit in the sands of North Africa, prayed three Rosaries a day. *Father Lamy*, a French diocesan pastor, never tired of praying the Rosary and recommended it as a powerful weapon against every danger: "When you walk the streets praying the Rosary, you have nothing to fear. You can walk feeling safe." He went so far as to guarantee that if necessary the Virgin Mary would send an angel to rescue her clients. And how many other holy priests of that era manifested a like devotion!

On April 25, 1981, Bishop Boleslas Sloskans was buried, aged 88. He had been secretly consecrated in Russia in 1926 by Bishop d'Herbigny. But he soon became a marked man and was arrested in 1927. The Soviets moved him from prison to prison, seventeen in all, and subjected him to inhuman torture.

Father Werenfried van Staaten, who had known him, said: "His spirit never broke. He would pray and meditate on the Way of the Cross and the mysteries of the Rosary. One day a guard, puzzled at the Bishop's constant smile, asked in wonderment: 'You are happy!' 'Yes,' said the Bishop, 'because I am completely free, which is not the case with you.' "

Example of the Lay People

Lay people of all ranks of life have also been known for their devotion to the Rosary. The French *General Drouot*, "wise old man of Napoleon's armies," would pray the Rosary at a gun emplacement on the Tuileries, *Daniel O'Connell* in a corner of the English Parliament, and the eminent physician *Récamier* on the way to his patients. The story is told that one day *Robert Schumann* rose to speak in a parliamentary debate, absent-mindedly still holding the Rosary in his hand, which he had been fingering in his vest pocket.

Also known is the life-long devotion to the Rosary of commanders of the army *Marshal Foch* and *Marshal Leclerc.*

In a major seminary of France (Langres), the kitchen help used to pray the Rosary while peeling vegetables. Their fingers were occupied, so they counted off the Hail Marys.

A priest-confrere sent us the testimony of a "convert of Mary." This follower of Mary tells of meditating on the mysteries of the Rosary from morning till night, walking about, riding the subway, and wherever he goes. Indeed, his daily life is the Rosary, and everything else is incidental.

In our day, we are aware that in retreat houses some persons succeed in reciting many Rosaries daily, as many as a dozen, as did Padre Pio. Such devotion is obviously exceptional, but it shows that it is not terribly difficult to recite at least one Rosary.

St. Louis-Marie Grignion de Montfort assures us:

> Those who faithfully do so
> Advance rapidly,
> Live perfectly,
> Die peacefully,
> And rise surely
> To eternal life.

Example of John Paul II

To conclude this chapter we might best cite the example of Pope John Paul II.

From the beginning of his pontificate he expressed his predilection for the Rosary. He led the recitation every evening on the Vatican Radio, whenever possible. He urged devotion to it on every occasion.

It is clear that for him, as for numerous saints of whom we have mentioned a few, regular contemplation of the mysteries of the faith in the setting of the Rosary constituted the spiritual atmosphere in which he moved. It afforded him wisdom, strength, and peace, as well as that apostolic attraction that wins the people.

His example is one more proof—and a most eloquent one—that contrary to some ill-considered and peremptory assertions, the Rosary is as relevant today as it was in the time of St. Pius V, Leo XIII, St. Pius X, and Paul VI.

Chapter 9

THE ROSARY:
PRAYER OF THE CHURCH

ALTHOUGH the part played by St. Dominic in the history of the Rosary is uncertain, there is no doubt that it was his spiritual sons of the 15th century who contributed most to its structuring and promotion. That is why the Popes have turned to the Dominicans for its continued promulgation.

In a letter of September 20, 1892, to the Master-General of the Dominican Order, Pope Leo XIII brought this papal desire to their attention. And in the Apostolic Constitution *Ubi Primum* of October 2, 1898, he made it official, entrusting them with the express mission of the Rosary.

For his part, as we have seen, Leo XIII fostered this devotion in an extraordinary manner. He says, for example, in one of his encyclicals:

"For a long time we have wanted to place the salvation of human society in increased veneration of the Blessed Virgin as in a refuge that is absolutely sure. To this end we have never ceased to promote among the faithful of Christ the habit of praying the Rosary of Mary."

The result of these combined efforts has been such a popularization of the Rosary that it is not merely a devotion of private groups but, in some sense, has truly become a devotion of the Church.

Can it be called a liturgical devotion?

Pope Paul VI faced the question when preparing his Apostolic Exhortation on Devotion to the Blessed Virgin Mary *(Marialis cultus)* of February 2, 1974. According to Father Galot, S.J., who briefed reporters on March 22, 1974, his mind was as follows:

"Some have asked that the Rosary be declared a liturgical prayer. It is true that in many respects it harmonizes well with the Liturgy. Nevertheless, it must not be confused with the Liturgy nor be superimposed on it, as has sometimes happened in the past. The Rosary should preserve its own character as an exercise of piety well designed to bring about better understanding and better living of the Liturgy."

The matter could scarcely be expressed any better, and such praise is most heartening. In short, we can concur in the assessment made by Pope John XXIII on September 29, 1961: "The Rosary has attained the rank of a great public prayer."

Reasons for This Approbation

What are the *reasons* behind this regard for the Rosary?

Cardinal Garrone examines them in his book, *Mary, Today and Yesterday*, published in 1977. Why, he asks, does the Rosary have such appeal for the Church?

Because it is a prayer in which the Church recognizes her faith and her life. In his own words:

"The place given the Rosary in the Church may seem surprising and is something to think about. The Church obviously regards it as a good of hers and defends and promotes it with untiring fervor. The Council, in its chapter on the Blessed Virgin, all but mentioned it. The Rosary forms part of the devotions to the Virgin Mary which the Church 'recognizes' because she finds it an expression of her beliefs and her way of life. The Rosary is certainly considered by the Church as a treasure."

The Cardinal goes on to say that it is easy to see why it could not be otherwise, and gives five reasons.

Loved by Common People and Fosters Faith

1. First, because of the love which the *common people* in the Church have for the Rosary. True, this love is sometimes expressed in ways that are a little inept or ill-conceived. But that is no argument against the Rosary, which has always been exposed to the light disdain of those whom Pascal calls the "half-learned," cynics who harp on the superficial aspects of things and miss the deeper implications. That the Rosary is loved by the common people is, in the eyes of the Church, a good sign. Their love, as a matter of fact, springs from a real understanding of the things of faith.

2. Secondly, the Rosary fosters *faith.*

It is a prayer concerning faith, a contemplative prayer. Newman wrote: "The great power of the Rosary is that it makes a prayer of a Creed." He also notes that "in a sense, the Creed is already a prayer and an act of homage to God."

The Rosary has the advantage of covering the entire range of the mysteries of our faith, mysteries which ultimately are one. The Church's preference, in fact, is for the complete Rosary (twenty decades), and we should never underestimate the great advantage of being able to hold, as Newman said, "one's entire faith in the hand."

A Humble Prayer of Petition

3. The Rosary is a humble *prayer of petition.* There is a conception of the spiritual life that would minimize the importance of petition in prayer, with a view to some love supposedly pure. But there is no such prayer, no prayer that does not imply the recognition of a want or insufficiency and appeal for God's help.

It is true that the Rosary stresses the aspect of petition. Some writers even think it stresses it too much and that this repetition does not accord with the counsel of the gospel (Mt 6:7). Such an opinion is completely erroneous. We have only to think of Jesus in the agony of the Garden, praying and, according to St. Mark, saying "the same words" over and over (Mk 14:39).

However, we can also see in this persistence the manner of the poor. Those whom Christ acknowledges and praises in the gospel are the poor and humble who press their petition until they are heard: like the Canaanite woman, or the widow in the parable of the corrupt judge. When repetition is the sign of deep distress together with a confidence that will not be disappointed, it is the sign of authentic prayer.

Missionary Power

4. Cardinal Garrone also adduces the "Marian factor" in the *missionary* activity of the Church, concerning which he says:

"Devotion to the Blessed Virgin, the Rosary in particular, is essentially missionary. One of the means to conversion is prayer, that first grace never lacking. The Rosary is specially suited to this purpose. It combines petition with contemplation of the mysteries. A prayer of this sort is an education in the faith and one of the surest and most effective ways to conversion. The Rosary is missionary by nature."

An all-too-little known illustration of the missionary effectiveness of the Rosary comes from Bishop Bataillon, apostle of the Papuans and member of the Marist Congregation:

"As soon as I arrived on the island I dedicated it to Mary. The mission seemed a failure, when I turned to the Rosary. It was my last resort. This devotion was embraced with an eagerness that was truly extraordinary. I do not believe there is a single parish where, proportionately, the Rosary is prayed as much as in our small mission. Before my arrival this island was, by all accounts, the worst in all Oceania. Now it is the model."

Maternal Role of Mary

5. The Cardinal's last reason why the Church thinks so highly of the Rosary is that it acquaints us with the

spiritual *motherhood of Mary.* We may be excused here for citing him at length:

"If the Church loves the Rosary, it is because it affords excellent training as regards the Motherhood of Mary, and especially as regards her motherly role of instructress in prayer.

"One has said nothing about the Rosary if the part that Mary plays in it has not been emphasized. Her role is maternal. In the Rosary we learn to treat her as our mother and day by day we grow in our filial relationship toward her. We learn to benefit, more and more, from the gift God made to us through St. John, at the foot of the cross.

"The Rosary teaches us to talk with Mary as we talk with our mother, opening our heart to her in humility and love and so acquiring the attitude of soul fundamental for the Kingdom of God.

"The Rosary, through the Virgin Mary, brings us closer to Jesus. Every mystery evokes an image of Christ in one of the moments of his redemptive action. It is to him that we are led, through Mary. His mysteries are brought closer to home by being couched in a Marian vocabulary. Not only are they no longer mere abstract truths, but they are viewed through Mary's inner life, where they were received and experienced.

"Ultimately, as the example of Lourdes and Bernadette makes clear, it is the Father to whom we are referred. There is something marvelously significant in the simple account of this young Saint, showing us the lips of the Virgin moving at the moment of the Our Father. The soul of Mary and the soul of her Son unite in Christ to bring to the Father the homage of adoration and love, which is like the last word of our faith and our Christian calling.

"It is certainly difficult to imagine another instrument of prayer both so simple and so powerful, so correct and so conformed to the essential of doctrinal truth.

"In order to understand what the Virgin Mary means to the Church and how the Church wants us to conduct ourselves toward Mary, there is no better way than reflecting on what the Rosary is and, above all, making use of it."

These citations express perfectly the sense of what we have been saying throughout this work.

Conclusion

We conclude the chapter with two observations:

1. Priests and faithful who look askance at the Rosary undoubtedly do not know it for what it truly is. One hopes that the esteem in which the Church holds it will, by the grace of God, lead them to more just appreciation.

2. It is important that promoters of the Rosary, even though specially named to the task, resist the temptation to manipulate it to suit their fancy, as though ultimate authorities. The Church has its stated preferences and directives on the subject. Humble preachers of the Rosary will bear them in mind.

Chapter 10

THE MYSTERY OF THE ROSARY

The Rosary: Marian Prayer

EVERYTHING said so far proves that the Rosary is a prayer of exceptional merit. So exceptional, in fact, that no matter how much we analyze it, the Rosary retains its mystery. Hence the title of this work (and chapter) is quite appropriate, even though at first there may be some question.

There is indeed a mystery of the Rosary, and not only its mysteries. When we speak of the mysteries of the Rosary, in the plural, the reference is to the great events in the life of our Lord, his birth, life, death, and resurrection. It is certain that these—the Incarnation, the Passion, the Resurrection—are mysteries, deep and basic to our faith, and we shall never have finished probing them in the spirit of contemplative prayer.

In principle, this contemplative prayer should be a matter of course. The Incarnation, together with its ramifications, is such a stupendous reality that there is nothing better than to have it always before us in continual outpouring of faith and love, so far at least as daily tasks allow.

The Rosary, however, is not simply a meditation on the great mysteries of salvation. It is this meditation but as related to the Virgin Mary. It is essentially a Marian prayer. The Hail Marys are addressed to her, and it is through her that we go to her divine Son, through her that we savor the joys of the sacred Infancy and Public Life, are grieved by the sufferings of the Passion and gladdened by the Resurrection.

This is so true that even historical events of the gospel in which she is not named, e.g., the agony of Jesus, his scourging, etc., are perceived and contemplated through her, with the same sort of feelings and emotions she must have experienced at the time.

The Mystery of the Rosary

If we consider this closely, we must admit that there is a mystery involved, a phenomenon that cannot be explained rationally.

Indeed, if we examine the makeup of the Rosary with a purely critical eye, we are hard put to see that the Blessed Virgin holds *such a preponderant position in it*. We would conclude that it is more in conformity with God's plan to address ourselves directly to Christ. After all, he it is who was made man, who died for us, and who rose again to open heaven for us—it was not the Blessed Virgin, who is only his collaborator in this work of Redemption and was herself saved by him.

Admittedly, we can find *good reasons* to justify this uninterrupted invocation of Mary. We can argue, for example, that as the Mother of Jesus she was with him in every circumstance of his childhood and hidden life and that she contributed to our salvation through her sharing in his redemptive sufferings.

However, the critical mind, based on logic alone, can always object that this does not suffice to make Mary the center of our prayer in the Rosary, that doing so is an abuse, and that we should address Christ directly.

Role of the Holy Spirit in the Church

What is the explanation for the Rosary having come to be an essentially Marian prayer? Since mere logic does not account for it, we are led to another source, the mysterious action of the Holy Spirit in the history of the Church.

The Holy Spirit does not enlighten believers by dint of syllogistic reasoning. The Holy Spirit has his own, inward way of leading pure souls to the truth. He guides them by means of a spontaneous instinct, a kind of supernatural taste and intuition which St. Thomas calls *connatural* grasp of the truth. And when there is question of venerating the Virgin Mary, *this instinct seems infallible*, as seen at Ephesus, when the divine motherhood of Mary was defined.

The special place which the Christian people have always accorded the Mother of God, especially since the Council of Ephesus, is a striking fact. Their devotion to her *has grown steadily through the centuries*. The medieval liturgy gave them an example, producing in her honor Offices and hymns of great beauty.

But the people went further, particularly in those long sequences of Marian salutations which lie at the origin of the Rosary. We have seen how this movement grew and formed, until it became the soundly structured prayer which, over the centuries, popes have so often and so warmly recommended.

It is not possible to imagine that a devotion so officially authenticated could be an aberration. The Holy Spirit cannot abandon the Church in such a vital matter. Moreover, heaven itself miraculously intervened to the same effect, at the Marian apparitions of the 19th and 20th centuries. There the Rosary is highly honored, whether expressly recommended by Mary or silently held in her hand as a sign of encouragement.

Adherence of the Faithful

The Christian people of the past were not mistaken. They embraced this most simple yet most fruitful form of prayer. Today again, they remain impervious to the scoffing of the pseudo-learned who reject the Rosary outright or tamper with it to the point of rendering it unrecognizable.

In the words of St. Louis-Marie Grignion de Montfort: "I know of no better way to determine if individuals are of God than by finding out if they love to pray the Hail Mary and the Rosary" (*True Devotion*, no. 251).

Superabundance of Divine Generosity

With any mystery it is permissible to look for its grounds and theological "suitabilities." As regards the Rosary and its development in the Church, two fundamental reasons, both theological, suggest themselves: (1) superabundance of divine generosity, and (2) maternal role of Mary.

The superabundance of the divine generosity is, no doubt, the principal reason.

The generous person gives unstintingly. The height of generosity is to give all. This has happened more than once. Wealthy nobles, great landowners, inheritors of family fortunes, people like these have given all to the poor or to works of religion in order to follow Christ in his poverty.

Once they have taken this heroic step, humanly speaking they are left with nothing.

God, by contrast, is so rich that his liberalities never leave him poorer. The more he gives, the more he is able to give. And he gives more generously according as he has nothing to fear from those whom he makes partners in his action, because he is the sole source of every good. When he enables created beings to be creators on their level, it is he who fills their hands with gifts for distribution.

These ideas are founded in philosophy as well as in theology. God is absolute Being, from which it follows (as philosophy can demonstrate) that all other beings in the material and spiritual universe come from him and depend on him, somewhat as the sun's rays depend upon the sun.

This is true at every degree in the hierarchy of beings. It is true in Christ himself. As St. Augustine explains, Christ as man received all from his Father. He could not merit the Incarnation, a purely free gift. Only after the fact could he merit in his capacity as the God-Man. But he was always mindful, as man, of his total dependence on the Father. Hence, he regularly gave thanks to the Father for all his blessings and prayed as often as his ministry allowed.

By the same token, God the Father could have no fear of losing the prerogatives he lent his Son. He could give him absolute dominion of our universe, knowing that the Son would not keep anything for himself but make a return of it in thanksgiving, until the time when he would hand back everything to his Father at the end of the world (see Col 1:15-20 and 1 Cor 15:24).

The Son, for his part, is not any more jealous of his collaborators than the Father is of him. Far from taking offense at seeing the faithful beseeching his Mother, he rejoices in it because he knows that she, too, makes a return of everything to God, reserving nothing for herself.

The Father allows the Son complete liberty in choosing the means most apt to touch our hearts and bend our stiff necks (since we are no better than the ancient Hebrews). Jacinta, the little girl who saw the Virgin at Fatima and who was recognized by the Church as Blessed on May 13, 2000, could say to her companion Lucy: "Tell everyone that God gives us his graces through the intermediary of the Immaculate Heart of Mary; that we should go to her for them; that the Heart of Jesus wants us to venerate with it the Immaculate Heart of Mary . . ." *(Memoirs of Sister Lucy)*.

The humble Virgin Mary, again like her Son, has obviously a preference for the poor and lowly, and for practices of devotion most within their grasp. This helps explain why, in the grace of the Holy Spirit, she has exerted herself in the development and promotion of the Rosary, a prayer so well adapted to their needs and capacities.

Maternal Role of Mary

A second clue to the mystery of the Rosary is the maternal action of Mary in regard to those who carry out this devotion in their life. St. Louis-Marie Grignion de Montfort states quite simply:

"As in the natural order a child should have a father and mother, so in the order of grace a true child of the Church should have God for Father and Mary for Mother" (*Secret of Mary*, no. 111).

God, no doubt, is as much Mother to us as he is Father. His mercy is boundless, and theoretically we have no need of intermediaries to form some notion of his tender love. But when there is question of revealed mysteries, theory must yield to facts. Since it was God's will to show us his love through Jesus and Mary, he had his reasons. He knew in particular that the feminine expression of love and compassion in the Heart of Mary was marvelously suited to touch our hearts.

That is why in the course of centuries he has mysteriously inclined the heart of the faithful toward Mary. How many sinners would have remained set in their ways but for the gentle figure of the Virgin beckoning them. How many Christians would have been less fervent without frequent recourse to her protection. And how many saints would have encountered more difficulties in their ascent to Calvary if they had not been sustained by her mother's hand and example.

Mystery of Vocation

After all is said, there remains an element of mystery in any veneration of Mary, and particularly in devotion to her Rosary. The attraction of Mary varies ad infinitum, from such giants as a St. Bernard of Clairvaux or a St. Maximilian Kolbe to more ordinary souls whose piety runs to three Hail Marys a day. How account for this diversity?

Spiritual writers recognize that not all souls are called to the same intensity of Marian life. This reverts to the mystery of grace and the infinite variation of its mode of operation.

Yet one thing we can be sure of, that grace does not suppress free will. If, then, fervent Christians are intellectually convinced of the advantages of devotion to Mary but do not feel attracted to it, they should not spring to the conclusion that this way is barred to them. Let them "knock at the door" of the Blessed Virgin. If they persevere, sooner or later the door will open.

Chapter 11

THE ROSARY AND THE EUCHARIST
Lesson of Marian Pilgrimages

IT is noteworthy that centers of Marian pilgrimages do not focus devotion exclusively on Mary. The further, and fundamental, orientation is to the Eucharist. At Lourdes, at Fatima, and elsewhere, processions of the Blessed Sacrament and festive Masses are climactic moments of pilgrimages.

This is as the Blessed Virgn herself would have it. She does not want the piety of the faithful to stop at her person but to proceed to her Son, and particularly to her Son present in the Eucharist, and through him to the eternal Father.

We ought to draw a lesson from this and in our lives bring the Rosary and the Eucharist together.

Admittedly, they are two essentially different realities. The Eucharist is a sacrament, the most sublime of all, toward which all others converge and from which all others derive their efficacy. The Rosary is only a sacramental.

But let us not forget the bond that links the Virgin of the Rosary to her Son. In all the mysteries it is to the Son of God that she leads us. In every Hail Mary it is on him that the salutations turn. Yet in the Rosary with its meditation we reach the Son of God only by faith.

We are not united with him sacramentally, as in the Eucharist.

However, the flow of contemplation and love which, through Mary, leads us to Jesus in the Rosary also leads us to desire him in the reality, infinitely mysterious, of the Eucharist.

That is why souls devoted to the Rosary are necessarily devoted to the Eucharist, and why they love to pray the Rosary before the tabernacle and, still more, before the Host in exposition in the monstrance.

Suggestions

For a long time, as Leo XIII had prescribed, the Rosary was recited in this way in the month of October, i.e., before the Blessed Sacrament exposed. Theoretically, this practice may be questionable, and critics probably contributed to its disappearance, almost everywhere. But here, as often in Christianity, facts carry more weight than theories.

Now, it is a fact that the presence of the Blessed Sacrament is a great help to prayer. And it is a fact, more particularly, that meditating on the mysteries of the Rosary in its presence can make them more real to us.

For example, as regards the Incarnation, we might meditate as follows:

1) The Word of God who became flesh in the womb of the Virgin is as truly present, though in a different manner, in the tabernacle.

2) When Mary, with Jesus now conceived in her, walked the road of Aïn Karim to her cousin Elizabeth, she was like a living monstrance, and she continues to set us an example of adoration in the obscurity of faith.

3) At Bethlehem Jesus was not more truly present than he is in the Eucharist; besides, we of today know much more about the Divinity of Christ than the shepherds and Magi did.

4) When Mary and Joseph presented the Child Jesus in the temple of Jerusalem, they were deeply moved by the holiness of the place, abode of the Most High. It was there that the resplendent ritual of Jewish worship unfolded. Yet what was offered to God consisted only of material things.

On the other hand, as spiritual writers point out, the day that Mary placed Jesus on the altar God received an Offering worthy of himself. And it can be said that ever since that first offering she has presented her Son to the Father in union with all priests who celebrate Mass.

5) The fifth joyful mystery suggests that we, too, go in search of Jesus. And, as then, we find him in our temples, thanks to the Eucharist.

The sorrowful mysteries offer less variety in their relation to the Holy Eucharist. Nevertheless, each of them declares with staggering realism the price our Lord paid in his bloody sacrifice and, therefore, in his unbloody sacrifice of the Mass. The presence of the Blessed Sacrament is a poignant reminder of this as we meditate on these mysteries.

Similarly association with the Eucharist can be shown in the glorious mysteries, for example by recalling that the divine Life which the Destroyer of death possesses in fullness is found in the consecrated Host; that the Ascension does not deprive us of the

Humanity of Jesus, because of the Eucharist; that this Sacrament and Sacrifice is an inexhaustible source of gifts of the Holy Spirit, and finally that Mary, by her assumption and coronation, is reunited with her Son in heaven whom she worshiped on earth under the appearances of consecrated Bread.

Earlier we quoted the following from St. Louis-Marie Grignion de Montfort:

"A soul that prays the Rosary every day will never become a formal heretic nor be deceived by the devil. This is a proposition I would seal with my blood."

The saint's categorical promise is even more assured if we pray the Rosary with reference to the Blessed Sacrament and, when possible, in its presence. Such contact with the eucharistic Presence brings the soul ever richer rewards of supernatural illumination, spiritual vitality, and blessedness.

Incomparable Superiority of Christianity

In a previous chapter, speaking of Oriental methods, a point was made of Christianity's superiority over other religions. Today more than ever, this needs to be brought home, especially in view of the ignorance afflicting those who look elsewhere for what they could find among us, who have not only incomparable forms of prayer like the Rosary but the reality of God's presence in the Eucharist.

For example, young men and women by the thousands have been going to India where they beg their daily bread and apply to gurus for the ways of holiness and happiness. Many of them were baptized in the

Catholic Church. But they know nothing about the spiritual resources of the Church. A respectable periodical interviewed some thirty such Europeans who had joined a Hindu monastery near Bombay. Among the findings:

"None of them seemed to know that the Church, as well as their guru, had ways of helping them find God, priests for instance. . . .

"Priests? You can never get to speak with them!

"And the Eucharist, where God gives himself to us?

"We were never told about that. Never."

In this respect, the author recalls one time when he helped to hear confessions. The penitential service, with individual confessions, took place in the chapel of a Catholic cultural center.

At this time there was much coming and going before the Blessed Sacrament. Not one of the children made the least sign of respect toward the Holy Eucharist. I was the only one to genuflect when passing before the tabernacle.

With such a state of affairs, how can we expect our young people to hold on to their Catholic faith, if indeed they ever had it? And whose fault is it?

If only they were trained in true Marian piety, at least in minimal praying of the Rosary, and instilled with living faith in the Eucharist, things would not be where they are.

Chapter 12

TECHNIQUE OF THE ROSARY

THE present form of the Rosary goes back several centuries. Has the time come for alterations, without prejudice to its essential character? This is what a number of writers, Dominicans among them, proposed some years ago.

The controversy that ensued testified to the popularity of the Rosary and the interest taken in it at all levels of the Catholic Church. For the moment these discussions have subsided. But certain problems remain. The purpose here is not to go into every detail but to consider some consequential matters which keep cropping up.

1. Translation and Role of the Hail Mary

Translation of the Hail Mary. Some translations of the Hail Mary are satisfactory. They need only a light touch here and there to be excellent.

On some points there is little consensus, however. Instead of "Hail, Mary" should we say "Rejoice, O Mary"? And "highly favored" for "full of grace"? There may be room for discussion here, and discussions have not been lacking.

However, pastoral priests, concerned about their people, point out that the Hail Mary, along with the Our

Father is the most widely used prayer, clung to even by nonpracticing members: the "prayer of the poor," as it has been called; and that if it were tampered with, many of them would be turned off. For this reason Paul VI decided that for now, translations should be left as they are. As a provisional solution, it was no doubt the wisest course.

Role of the Hail Mary. Some have proposed a deeper reform: suppression of the second part of the Hail Mary nine times out of ten, claiming that this prayer of petition intrudes on the meditative process.

Regarding this point, too, we have expressed disagreement. One argument of substance against it can be drawn from the Jesus Prayer (see Chapter 8). Everyone admits that this prayer is eminently favorable to contemplation. Yet in essence its structure is exactly like that of the Hail Mary: first, an act of faith (Lord, Jesus Christ), then a petition (be merciful to me, a sinner).

Passing remark. If small groups would like to innovate among themselves, there is nothing to stop them. But it should be done in such a way that one still recognizes the Rosary—or admit that it is something else.

2. Meditation of the Mysteries

A second problem remains to be resolved: how to associate the Hail Mary with contemplation or meditation of the mysteries. If attention is focused on every word of the Hail Mary, how can we think of the mystery? And if the mystery absorbs us, can we still think on the words?

This, undoubtedly, is an obstacle to be overcome. The ancient Jews, viewing God's wonderful works, were completely immersed in contemplation. And the first Christians simply meditated on the gospel. For centuries no one could have foreseen the appearance of a form of prayer in which contemplation of God's marvels would proceed by way of Mary's soul and heart. That it did appear, and prosper, pertains to the "mystery" of the Rosary of which we spoke in Chapter 10.

To many people, nevertheless, it is confusing. How deal with the problem?

In a word, by recourse to the "reconstitution of places" before pronouncing the words. There are a number of practical ways to do this. For example:

1. Picturing to ourselves the mystery as we begin the decade.

2. Adding a clause to each Hail Mary: ". . . blessed is he who took flesh in you; who was in you at the Visitation; whom you conceived, etc."

3. Reading, before beginning the decade, a passage from the gospel relating to it. Or failing that, pausing a few moments for intense thought about the mystery.

4. Some booklets on the Rosary propose a text for each Hail Mary. This would be most helpful to meditation but involves a good deal of time. It is a luxury we might permit ourselves now and then, in periods of flagging attention or enthusiasm.

5. Also—since nothing is negligible in this domain— when praying the Rosary while we are traveling or doing our work, it is sometimes surprising to relate what we are seeing or doing to what Jesus and Mary

saw and did. For example, in most countries there are sites or regions reminiscent of sites and regions in Palestine. But apart from that, many of our activities and states of mind bear analogy with the models contemplated.

Drawing these comparisons particularizes the realities grasped by faith. And it is an excellent way of keeping the mind in focus and making the connection, so to speak, between our material world and the supernatural world.

Readers almost anywhere have available practical aids to praying and appreciating the Rosary. They can visit or write to centers of Marian devotion, particularly Dominican houses and convents, all of which are somehow engaged in the apostolate of the Rosary. There they will find ample choice of books, magazines, pamphlets, and audio-visual aids adapted to every age group and every taste.

CONCLUSION

IN recent years many priests and Christians have lost the taste for authentic prayer, and particularly for the Rosary. Instead, they bury themselves in secular activity and so serve the cause of sectarian groups who claim a monopoly of the spiritual life.

The essential mission of Christianity is to lead souls to God: "Seek first his kingship over you, his way of holiness, and all these things will be given besides" (Mt 6:33).

It is in living their faith, and in proportion to their living it, that Christians promote both the conversion of the world and its temporal good.

Living the faith. The Rosary, on the authority of the Church, is a privileged instrument of nurturing the faith and advancing the Christian life—on condition that we have a mature understanding of it and, above all, practice it diligently.

Perhaps these pages will contribute to this understanding and foster the appreciation the Rosary deserves.

The Five
Joyful Mysteries

(Said on Mondays and Saturdays, the Sundays of Advent, and Sundays from Epiphany until Lent.)

1. The Annunciation — *Luke 1:28.*
2. The Visitation — *Luke 1:42.*
3. The Nativity — *Luke 2:7.*
4. The Presentation — *Luke 2:28.*
5. Finding in the Temple — *Luke 2:46.*

1. The Annunciation
For the love of humility.

2. The Visitation
For love of neighbor.

4. The Presentation
For the virtue of obedience.

3. The Nativity
For the spirit of poverty.

5. Finding in the Temple
For the virtue of piety.

93

The Five
Luminous Mysteries

(Said on Thursdays.)

1. The Baptism of Jesus — *Matthew 3:13-17.*
2. Christ's Self-Manifestation at Cana — *John 2:1-11.*
3. Proclamation of the Kingdom of God — *Mark 1:15; Matthew 5:1-11.*
4. The Transfiguration — *Matthew 17:1-8.*
5. Institution of the Eucharist — *Matthew 26:26-30.*

1. The Baptism of Jesus
For living Baptismal promises.

2. Christ's Self-Manifestation at Cana
For doing whatever Jesus says.

4. The Transfiguration
Becoming a new person in Christ.

3. Proclamation of the Kingdom
For seeking God's forgiveness.

5. Institution of the Eucharist
For active participation at Mass.